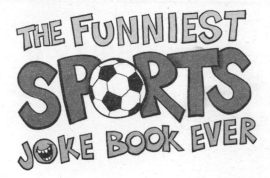

THE FUNNIEST SPORTS JOKE BOOK EVER

Collect them all!

THE FUNNIEST SPORTS JOKE BOOK EVER

By Joe King

Illustrated by Nigel Baines

First published in 2020 by
Andersen Press Limited
20 Vauxhall Bridge Road
London SW1V 2SA
www.andersenpress.co.uk

2 4 6 8 10 9 7 5 3 1

British Library Cataloguing in Publication Data
available.

ISBN 978 1 78344 964 4

Printed and bound in Great Britain by
Clays Limited, Elcograf S.p.A.

Olympic-sized Laughs

Where do spiders stage their Olympics?

Web-ley Stadium

Why aren't the Olympics held in outer space?

Because there's no atmosphere

What's the fastest sport at the Olympics?

Quicket

Why are Olympic stadiums so hot after an event has finished?

Because all the fans have left

If laziness was an Olympic sport, I'd try to come fourth so I wouldn't have to walk up the podium.

Why did lots of runners slip over during the first ever Olympics?

Because they were held in Grease

Why couldn't the Olympian listen to music?

Because she'd just broken the record

How are scrambled eggs like a losing Olympian?

They've both been beaten

**How was the pole
vaulting event?**

*Great, the teams really took the
competition to new heights*

**Why did the stupid
tug-of-war team lose?**

They pushed

**Why do Scandinavian
countries do well in races?**

They're close to the Finnish line

**How do you confront a
fear of hurdles?**

Just get over it

**What did they call Dracula
when he won a gold medal?**

A champire

**Which athletes are the
warmest?**

Triple jumpers

Why are athletes so talkative?
They've got lots to discus

**What's a gymnast's
favourite dessert?**
Banana split

**What do boxers like
to drink at parties?**
Punch

**Are you excited
that they're adding
breakdancing as an
Olympic sport?**

*I'm head
over heels!*

Someone was arrested for plotting to steal all the gold from the Olympics.
They'd have gotten away with it, if it weren't for those medaling kids.

What's the point of archery?

It's the bit that goes into the target

What do you get if you cross a fencer with the Invisible Man?

A bout like nobody's ever seen

What do gymnasts practice on in hot countries?

Sunbeams

Aquatic Amusements

What kind of race is never run?

A swimming race

What do you call fishing when you don't catch any fish?

Drowning worms

What's the best animal to take out sailing?

A giraft

Why should you do the backstroke after lunch?

Because you're not supposed to swim on a full stomach

What goes in pink and comes out blue?

A swimmer in winter

Why did the swimming teacher jump into the pool?

She wanted to test the water

Why are boaties so bad-tempered?

Because they love to row

There's a millionaire who has two swimming pools, but one's always empty. It's for people who can't swim

**What did the sea say
to the swimmer?**

Nothing, it just waved

**Where do swimmers
clean themselves?**

They wash up on the shore

**Our rowing team lost their race.
It was quite the oar-deal.**

**Which vegetables are banned
during the sailing?**

Leeks

**What did the swimmer say when
he hit a concrete wall?**

'Dam!'

What ships are crewed by vampire sailors?

Blood vessels

What swimming stroke goes well with jam?

The butter-fly

Which sea creatures are the strongest?

Mussels

Swimming's a confusing sport. Sometimes you do it for fun, sometimes you do it not to die.

What time does the swimming start?
At water past the hour

Where are ghost regattas held?
The Dead Sea

Where does the water polo team have celebratory meals?
At the pool table

Having a Ball

Why are kangaroos good at basketball?

They always make the jump shots

What kinds of stories do netballers tell?

Tall tales

Are you going to watch the match tomorrow?

No need, I can tell you the score before the game starts.

Really, what is it then?

Nil-nil!

Why isn't Cinderella any good at sports?

Because she's always running away from the ball

Why do footballers like footballs?

They get a kick out of them

Did you hear about the stupid goalkeeper?

He saved a penalty but let it in on the action replay

'Why didn't you stop the ball?'

'I thought that's what the net was for.'

What do netballers and babies have in common?

They both wear bibs

What did the goalie say to the ball?

'Catch you later!'

Why was the ball dribbling?

You'd dribble too if your head was bouncing off the floor

Why was the stegosaurus such a good volleyball player?

Because she could really spike the ball

**Which sport requires
the most effort?**

Rugby – you really have to try

**A rounders fielder wondered
why the ball kept getting
bigger and bigger.
Then it hit him.**

**What's a baseball player's
least favourite Star Wars film?**
The Umpire Strikes Back

**What did one dodgeball
say to the other?**

'See you round.'

**Where are criminal squash
players judged?**

In a squash court

**Which player on a netball
team has the best
sense of smell?**

The scenter

Where do ghosts play golf?

On a golf corpse

Why is basketball the messiest sport?

Because the players dribble all over the court

What happened when the pencil lacrosse team played the pen lacrosse team?

It ended in a draw

Which baseball player holds the team's water?

The pitcher

I've just started playing rugby. I thought I was doing really well, but all my coach ever says is 'Nice try!'

Witty Winter Sports

Why shouldn't you tell jokes while ice-skating?

The ice might crack up

**What's the hardest
part of skating?**

The ice

**How popular has Olympic
curling become?**

It's sweeping the nation

**What is the best part of a
figure skater's party?**

The icing on the cake

**What do figure skaters
say when they meet
someone new?**

Something to break the ice

**Why don't penguins
play sport?**

Because there is snow balls

**How does Jack Frost
get to work?**

By icicle

**How can bobsleighing lead to
a life of crime?**

It's a slippery slope

Why was the figure skater so unapproachable?

She was always giving people the cold shoulder

What sport is a Christmas tree good at?

Alpine skiing

Which Winter Olympians have the best hair?

The curling team

What often falls at the Winter Olympics but never gets injured?

Snow

**Which athletes are
the best dressed?**

The ski jumpers

**Which team is
always angry?**

The cross country skiers

**Why did the skier decide to
swap sports?**

Because he was snowboard

**Which winter sport is the
most expensive?**

The buy-athlon

Why does toilet paper like alpine skiing?

It's the fastest way to the bottom

Why is the Winter Olympic lost property office always calling people called Robert?

Because they've found Bob's sleigh

Why are Winter Olympians so popular?

They're really cool

What's the most popular breakfast cereal at the Winter Olympics?

Frosties

What disease can you catch from scared ice hockey players?

Chicken pucks

What event celebrates the end of the Winter Olympics?

A Snow Ball

Tennis Ticklers

Which athletes make the best waiters?

Tennis players, because they're brilliant at serving

Why are fish terrible tennis players?

They don't like getting close to the net

Why are tennis players bad at relationships?

Because love means nothing to them

Why are tennis matches so loud?

The players are always raising a racquet

When does a tennis match end?

When it's Wimble-done

When do tennis players go to bed?

Ten-ish

What do you call a girl standing in the middle of a tennis court?

Annette

Where do tennis players dance?

At a tennis ball

Where do they make films about tennis?

Volleywood

What's a horse's favourite sport?

Stable tennis

Which Bible story mentions tennis?

The one where Moses serves in Pharaoh's court

Which comic book character is the best at sports?
Tennis the Menace

What comes before tennis?
Nine-is

Why don't tennis players ever change lightbulbs?
They won't admit when they're out

Why are people so critical of tennis players?
Because they've got many faults

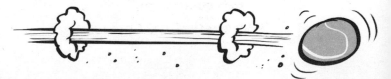

What should you serve but not eat?
Tennis balls

Which state do American tennis players train in?
Tennis-see

Which tournament never closes?
The Australian Open

**Why are umpires
good on the phone?**

*They're used to making
tough calls*

**Why was the apple so
successful in tournaments?**

It was seeded

**Why does Wimbledon
employ birds?**

For the Hawkeye

Athletic Animals

Why was the chicken given a red card?

For fowl play

Which insects aren't good in goal?

Fumblebees

I did say I was much better on the wing...

What did the bumblebee striker say?

'Hive scored!'

Why can't dogs dance?

They've got two left feet

**Why should you be careful
when playing against a team
of big cats?**

They might be cheetahs

**Did you hear about the sheep
who's a champion hurdler?**

They call him the woolly jumper

How do fireflies start a race?

'On your marks, get set, glow!'

**Why couldn't the bear
run in the marathon?**

It's not part of the human race

In which direction do chickens run?

Cluck-wise

What do T-rex referees announce?

The dino-score

What do you call a pig who plays rugby?

A ball-hog

Why didn't the big cat win the race?

He didn't cross the lion

What animal is the best at cricket?

A bat

What's an insect's favourite sport?

Cricket

Why don't centipedes go bowling?

The alley never has enough shoes

What position do turkeys play in rounders?

First baste

Which animals always have the most goals?

Score-pions

What's a pig's favourite karate move?

A pork chop

What's a bee's favourite sport?

Rugbee

Cycling
Side-splitters

What book has the best information about bikes?

An encyclopedia

Last winter, I saw someone up to their neck in snow. I asked if she needed help, but she said, 'That's OK, I'm on my bicycle.'

What do you call an artist who sculpts with bicycle parts?

Cycleangelo

Why isn't it safe for bears to ride bikes?

They don't have thumbs so they can't ring the bell

My friend rode into a tree the other day. Luckily he was OK – the bark was worse than his bike.

I don't know much about the Tour de France, but it seems like the best way to win is to wear a yellow T-shirt.

Why couldn't the bike finish the race?

It was two-tyred

Did you read about the bike that kept causing accidents at the Tour de France?

It was a vicious cycle

Why did the kid take his bicycle to bed?

He didn't want to walk in his sleep

My friend's started cycling 100km a day. It's been a week and nobody has a clue where she is!

Why can't you take a nap during the Tour de France?

If you snooze, you lose

How did the bike feel when it got a puncture?

Deflated

My dog is such a troublemaker, he's always barking at people on a bicycle.

What are you going to do?

I suppose I'll have to take away his bike.

What dinosaur can ride a bike?

The velo-ciraptor

What do you get if you cross a bike with a flower?

Bicycle petals

What is the cheapest type of bicycle?

A penny-farthing

My new bike wheels were missing something in the middle. When I phoned to complain, they put me straight through to their spokesperson.

Why was the bike's wheel haunted?

It had spooks in it

Why did the cyclist's prize acceptance speech bore everyone to sleep?

He kept velo-droning on

My bike chain rusted, then lots of other things started going wrong.
It was a chain reaction.

Ridiculous Runners

How did the barber win the marathon?

He took a short cut

When is a runner not a runner?

When they turn into a driveway

What runs around a field but never moves?

A fence

What is harder to catch the faster you run?

Your breath

Who was the fastest runner in history?

Adam, he was the first in the human race

Why did the forgetful girl take up running?

To jog her memory

What should you do if you split your sides laughing?

Run until you get a stitch

What do you call someone who runs behind a car?

Exhausted

Did you hear about the marathon runner who ran for three hours but only moved two feet?

That's fair enough, he only has two feet

What condiment do runners need when they're losing a race?

Ketchup

My friend told me she wants to take up cross-country running. I told her she should start with a small one, maybe Monaco.

What do sprinters eat before a big race?

Fast food

Did you hear about the married marathon runners who live in different countries?

They have a long-distance relationship

What is a runner's favourite school subject?

Jog-graphy

Prizewinning Puns

What lights up a stadium?
A match

Why don't artists ever win at sport?

They're always drawing

Why do boxers love jokes?

Because of the punch lines

Why did the ballerina quit?

Because it was getting tutu difficult

How does Dracula stay fit?
He plays batminton

I took the shell off my racing snail to speed him up. It only made him sluggish

What's the quietest game?
Bowling – you can hear a pin drop

Why is it a bad idea to listen to a match?

You'll burn your ear

Why did the netballer quit?

She'd lost her goal in life

How is our trampolining team doing?

Oh you know, they're up and down

Why do skeleton sports teams never win?

Because their hearts aren't in it

Is the trampolining team upset about its performance?

A bit, but they'll bounce back

What did the skier say as she began her race?

'It's all downhill from here!'

Why is string helpful to a losing team?

So they can tie the game

Why are rock climbers the bravest athletes?

Because they're boulder

Why did the golfer wear two pairs of trousers?

In case she got a hole-in-one

How is a cricket team similar to a pancake?

They both need a good batter

Why was there a ghost cheerleader?

To add a little team spirit

Why don't swimmers make good footballers?

Because they're always diving

One-one was a racehorse. Two-two was one too. One-one won one race, and two-two won one too.

Why do basketball players love biscuits with their tea?

Because they can dunk them

Why did the F1 champion always drive in reverse?

Because he knew the course backwards

I'd love a new boomerang for my birthday, but I can't seem to throw the old one away.

My dancing teacher told me there are only two things stopping me from becoming a great ballerina – my feet.

What do dentists and sports coaches have in common?

They both use drills

Why are referee retirement parties the best?

They love a good send-off

Why didn't the dog want to learn karate?

It was a boxer

Football Farces

What position do ghosts play?
Ghoul-keeper

Why should you marry a goalie?
Because they're keepers

What do footballers drink?
Penal-tea

Why couldn't the car play football?
Because it only had one boot

What do footballers and magicians have in common?
Hat tricks

Who scored the most goals in the Greek Mythology league?
The centaur forward

What would NASA use to make a space football pitch?

Astro-turf

Which part of a football stadium is different every match?

The changing rooms

How did the football pitch become a triangle?

Somebody took a corner

Why do footballers get upset at Christmas?

They get lots of red cards

Why did the ref snap her watch in two?

To let everyone know it was half-time

Why are good goalies so rich?

They're always saving

Did you hear about the useless goalkeeper?

When he missed a save he held his head in his hands – and dropped it!

**Why do referees seem
so cheery?**

*They're always whistling while
they work*

**Why did the butterfly flutter
along the side of the pitch?**

It was a winger

**Which league do potatoes
play in?**

The Premier-chip

**Did you hear about the time it
was raining football players?**

It was really teaming it down

Why were the footballers all jumping over ropes in training?

They were hoping to be the next skipper

Who can spot a good player at the same time as lighting a fire?

A scout

Why did the team play in the manager's living room?

It was a home game

Who arranges team transport?

The coach

Fighting Funnies

What do you call a goat that knows martial arts?

Karate kid

Does a match box?
No, but a tin can

How do you make a fruit punch?
Teach it to box

What did the zero say to the eight?
'Nice black belt!'

What do fighters say when they've tripped?
'I didn't fall, I was attacking the floor.'

I keep forgetting which martial arts are in the Olympics. It's a bit kung-fu-sing

What do you call an injured martial arts star?
Bruised Lee

What do you call a sheep doing karate?
A lamb chop

How can you tell someone with baggy trousers is bad at karate?
They haven't got any belts

What martial art do British people like?
Karatea

Did you enjoy the karate?
It was sensei-tional

What do you call someone who's just started judo?
A partial artist

What do you call a grandmother who knows karate?

A grandmartial artist

What do you call someone who's been knocked out?

A sore loser

'Coach, my sparring partner called in sick, can I train alone today?'

'Knock yourself out.'

Knock Knock

Knock knock
Who's there?
The guy who finished second
*The guy who finished
second who?*
Exactly

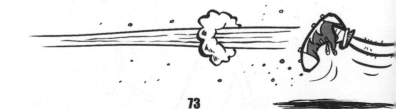

Knock knock
Who's there?
Dumbbell
Dumbbell who?
Dumbbell doesn't work so I had to knock!

Knock knock
Who's there?
Stopwatch
Stopwatch who?
Stopwatch you're doing and open this door!

Knock knock
Who's there?
Hula
Hula who?
Yes, I'd love to Hula Hoop

Knock knock
Who's there?
Iran
Iran who?
Iran over here to tell you this

Knock knock
Who's there?
Canoe
Canoe who?
Canoe come and watch the boat race?

Knock knock
Who's there?
Everybody
Everybody who?
Everybody was kung fu fighting

Knock knock
Who's there?
Money
Money who?
My knee hurts when I run

Knock knock
Who's there?
Tennis
Tennis who?
Tennis my favourite number

Knock knock
Who's there?
Annie
Annie who?
Annie body want to come to the match?